Corinne

under the Sun

May You find Light in these Words

poems by

Glenis Redmond

Yours - N - Verse,

2014

MAIN STREET RAG PUBLISHING COMPANY
CHARLOTTE, NORTH CAROLINA

Cover art by Lynn Greer © 2002, *Determination*.
Author photo by Daniel Perales

Acknowledgements

These poems appeared first in the following publications:

Novello Press: "I Didn't Have My Colors Done"
New Life Journal: "She," "Birthdays"
Black Arts Quarterly: "She", "Z," "A Simple Act,"
    "A Slave Named Patience," "Sister Complex,"
Asheville Citizen Times: "Crows,"
Creations: "A Salute to Miracles,"
Emrys Journal: "White Flight,"
Winding Road Anthology: "Birthdays,"
Heartstone: "Burying the Dead,"
Fem Spec: "Scripted Hope," "Train," and "Lonely Girl,"
African Voices: "Sacrum,"
Obsidian III Literature in the African Diaspora:
    "The Unbearable Heat of South Carolina"
NC-Nonprofit Newsletter: "With Hands as well As Hearts"
Rivendell: Sacrum

Library of Congress Control Number: 2008933470

ISBN 13: 978-1-59948-133-3

Produced in the United States of America

Main Street Rag
PO Box 690100
Charlotte, NC 28227
www.MainStreetRag.com

This book stands on the shoulders of all my ancestors:

Rachel Rogers

Will Todd

Mabel Redmond

Willie Clifton Redmond

Johnny Clifton Redmond

Bee Redmond

Jannie Mae Morgan

Peter Todd

Doug Todd

Walter Bailey

And all those who died long before toiling in the red clay South and the coast of West Africa.

Ase',
Aho, and Amen

Contents

*There is a time for everything,
for every occupation under the sun*

a time for building,

SCRIPTED HOPE

Name every nighttime shadow.
Call them out
from every corner,
every crevice of the past.
Fill yourself with the power
named survival.
Your voice will flower silver
into a circle blooming
of compassionate witnesses,
burning trembling lights.
In the brightness
my voice becomes your voice,
your voice becomes mine.
Together, our voices form
a tight constellation of hope,
a calligraphy written in stars.

SHE

for Katie Latimore's Birthday, 101

Staring into Katie Latimore's eyes
I go straight into heaven,
rest in a blueness not here on earth.
With her I feel a certain mercy
I have never known.
She who grew hollyhocks, hibiscus, hydrangeas
and drew every stray cat in the county.
She who when not pickin' cotton,
grew vegetables in her yard,
fished in her spare time.
Rachel's daughter,
her mother born a slave,
bore sixteen children.
She in those desperate
dangerous times
held aspirations beyond the third grade
but never made it to that one-room schoolhouse.
Her knowledge was of another understanding,
a candle lit by the Almighty.
When I am wise I sit there and study her blue flame.
She smoked her Winston 100's,
inhaled a little,
letting the ash grow
until it fell like withered dreams beneath her feet.
She drank her Coca-Cola like medicine,
loved her potatoes sweet.
She made me thru my mother
thru and thru 'til
I am what I am
which is why even now,
I have a penchant for all things old;
never been particular about the new.

Glenis Redmond

It is why I gave birth to two incredibly old women.
I called them the Delaney sisters.
They came that way.
It is their spirit not their age.
She, my mother's mother, I am not calling a saint
but is there anybody living who would want
to walk in her shoes?
She has earned the glory of these words,
any respite they might bring.
She with her jet black ambition
tied to her hands,
her running feet
running thru cane fields,
cotton fields
always somebody else's
sharecropped land.
She deserves to run,
fight, do battle no more.
Lay it all down by the riverside.
But she is in the nursing home
with a fire, a rage burning bright.
I know because sometimes,
she won't let no white hand touch her.
When I leave there, She whispers,
"*Loves everybody, Chile,*
no matter how black,
how blue,
how brown,
or how white,
loves everybody."
For in those times
she was running water
clear, clean in that ingrown South

where revolution never happened,
not even now.
She was
IS the point of my inspiration,
showing me the revolution
is in staying alive.
After 101 years of living in the south,
I only know
She is closer to God
than anyone I have ever known.
Imagine coming from a shattered past,
heartache after heartache,
outlasting the death of almost everyone
for lasting 101 years.

What can I say to all those years of living?
What can anybody say to that woman
after 101 years and no monuments erected in her name,
each day a resurrection of struggle and the fight?
To the world I say, if we want to be well,
we sit down and listen with more than ears.

Glenis Redmond

CROWN GLORY

My hair is personal.
No, my hair is universal.
It has been around the block,
across the Atlantic
released in Medusa's locks.
Misunderstood, misrepresented
biblically noted, recorded and documented.
My crown and glory is a revolutionary tale,
a low country oak dripping stories like moss.
Telling of how my ancestors survived
and sometimes thrived a hot-comb history.
Curls pressed flat, steam shooting straight
to the head misery.
Or, a journey blanketed by shame,
with a bandanna shrieking the blues
of how we have gotten over
and always try to make it through.
Then,
chemicals laid flat
with a wide tooth comb
to stretch out the kink,
that eventually snaps back.
It always goes back
to the nap,
that's the power of being black,
the snap,
the tightly knitted bond, and strained links
having to be maintained every six weeks.
A billion-dollar industry upheld maintaining kinky locks
to ease the itchy scalp,
pressing in the promise of silk,
to ease the tension,
in the kitchen,

the back of the bus,
the restaurant,
the Jim Crow lines.
The painful strokes of the brush
beginning at the chin ending with,
hold still, girl. I ain't got time for your tenderhead.
I have gone to war.
I have been at war.
I am still at war everyday especially with those who declare
hair not political anymore.
Come withstand the stares, the ridicule, the judgment.
Cross the Mason-Dixon Line,
and express that unexamined, simpleminded sentiment.
Find those curious fingers crossing the boundary
of my locks without invitation,
those already strained strands
meant to be caressed only with the eyes
touched by invitation only
when asked to oil the patches of scalp,
where I sit back and relax
in a conditioned softness
which I have come to know
a wisdom I marinate in.
There is nothing like
falling into capable palms
releasing a powerful love
and attitude that says, *girl,*
I know what you been through
press your weary back
between familiar knees
take in a deep breath
leave your head to me.

Glenis Redmond

I lean back in this belief.
Feel firm in this strength.
Hold fast to the relief
that song of my locks remain free
to sing my story, our hairstory
telling how we strived for
fought for the dignity
to wear the beautiful woven legacy of the kinky crown.

SISTER COMPLEX

for my only sis, Velinda Simmons

I studied in her shadow.
Who needed the voice of *Vogue*?
I flipped the pages of *Velinda*,
the icon of my prepubescent angst.
She was everything in my father's eyes,
I was not.
She came here
via the Sahara of my mother's slopes;
progressed trippingly through life doe-eyed
and on her own volition.
Stacked with devout determination and purpose
she could write, could run, could draw, could dance
could *sang*
Lord have mercy, could she *sang,*
could cook, could sew, could dream, could travel.
Did I mention, she could run?
Naw, she could fly,
faster and higher than anyone I 've ever known.
You know I never stopped to ask the question why she could fly.
She just knew, and her world was seamless.
Satin went rough in her presence.
I remember slipping there
into her closet
hoping to find at least one run
or to see if one shoe heel
was crooked or creeled.
They were painfully perfect,
as if she walked on cirrus clouds by day
and traveled with the agility of shooting stars
in her dreams.
It was this day
I knew I would never be her

Glenis Redmond

plagued with the defect
of one leg one-eighth inch too short.
My shoes lived hard in the wearing.
Her Afro-wearing beauty was in sync with the Sixties.
Black and Latino brothers seemed to fall listless from trees
just to walk,
just to talk,
just to vibe off this Nubian Goddess.
Her beauty was world music
and you could hear congas, shekeres and kalimbas in each step;
and each step was a song.
It was she who first called Africa to me.
Lifting me up
out of my dogged Buster Brown blues
aligning vertebrae after vertebrae,
straightening spine,
taking me there
to the Motherland.
For it loved her,
adorning her at birth
with the marks of beauty
with a Cowrie-shell regalness
until she married dusk
and wore indigo as her cloak.
Under this dark wing,
she created a legion of teenage women,
The Afroettes,
dancing African in the sixties
to a mainstream world who'd never loved black.
These multi-brown rainbow-colored women taught me well.
I lived and breathed their caramel, ebony and onyx auras
exhaled their smoky essence.
Yes, to be clothed in African robes,

bend my back to God
and dance the prayers
of our many ancestors.
But, the entrance age was twelve, and I was nine.
Now when people see me under the lamplight
on the corner of Poetry and Prose,
they don't know I am not singing just my song.
I am nine
and I have been joined
by a tribe of dancing women
who have managed in this life
to not give over to *Vogue, Cosmo,* fairy tales
or any given channel on the silver TV screen.
I owe the aspiration of my hips
to my sister
who held a space for me;
a coming-out,
coloring me beautiful
with her brown rays.
In my heart
teaching me
a ritual of study,
a standard of beauty
not outside of myself.

Glenis Redmond

SHE CAN'T READ

She couldn't read,
much less read me
even look me up
like simple digits
listed in a telephone book.
She couldn't catch
the gist of my spine
standing straight,
my frame holding promise
pointing to that shimmering pond called sky
though I am sure she tried.

Saw herself reflected
as a swift dream,
a black swan gliding high,
migration was beneath her.
She gave flight
over to fight in the sixth grade.
In a perfect world
we'd all have wings.
But she couldn't read me
or spell it out
much less see me
with so much hate in her eyes
and she wasn't taking a chance on the flight.

THE COLOR PURPLE

The color purple is deep,
an ancient mantra deep.
A royal ribbon rolling deep,
rippling across the ages
carried by knowing seas deep
spitting out centuries of lost bones deep
held in the womb of the Atlantic deep
washing waves of where I come from deep
trouble I have seen,
felt, lived in, fought through, and
daily trying to keep my head above deep.
Flashing back lives
visions of my former selves
projecting futures of what I can be.
The color purple is a serious deep
a blue black deep getting at the source of disease deep
seeping way down beyond roots
to undo what's been done in evil's name.
Fingering black on black shame.
Shug looking at Celie spouting,
"You sho' is ugly."
The power of purple is necessary
The power of purple is contemporary.
It glorifies the black woman
"Sophia, Sophia, Sophia
ain't she pretty daddy?"
It is not Gone with the Wind.
It don't know nothin' 'bout birthin' no babies
just Celie pointing her hoodoo finger
at Mister on that buggy riding north
"Until you do right by me, everything you even think about gonna fail."
I pledge my allegiance to this color
because it takes a stand,

Glenis Redmond

does not sit down on the job,
does not flinch,
change its color,
straddle the fence,
takes stock,
but tells the whole story.
The flag I fly on my porch, bumper
and over my heart is human.
I pledge my allegiance to this flag
for every nation
is under God
when we overstand this lesson,
we will be indivisible
not invisible
when every person is respected,
there will liberty and justice for all.
My flag was not made with man-made hands.
It don't know nothin' about division, derision or lies.
My flag is about belief, about dignity,
about beauty growing rich in a springtime field,
budding a hue so strong human eyes
can't help but capture this soul rippling
purple tide of truth,
resonating in a realm, *all things are possible.*
This purple anthem blares blues, struts jazz
chants in West African tongues
backed with the brown mouth of Mahalia's gospel.
This purple don't walk, don't jog, it runs
bleeds true because it is on a mission.
It don't need no permission to dance
it does a victory stomp
the south African *Toyi-Toyi*
championing for the underdog

because purple is queen
of the disenfranchised,
the poor,
the homeless,
the raped,
the falsely accused,
the motherless child,
children with no daddies.
The color purple is a blue black badge of courage
carrying a history lesson an endless ribbon
shouting truth to all lies.
We did not begin at the cotton crop.
And we don't end at hip-hop.
This ribbon does a crisscross
double backs into joy
rooted in a strong song
beginning in the motherland
carried deep in the griot's heart.
How we were once stars
and carried this sky wisdom in our hearts
and mother earth's knowledge in our souls,
while a common language blessed our tongues
and graced the carriage of our tired feet
crossing over padding the message
we will always go through
but we will always get over
the color purple is a story written
in the sky
in indelible ink
you can't enslave a wave
there's no end to its flow.

Glenis Redmond

HOOD HIGH

Tribute to Jeffery

He holds the hood high
higher than I ever could or would.

I am fourth out of five children
born to Johnny and Jeanette
the only offspring born to their native state.

It should of been me
It should of been me flying the navy blue flag sky high
lifting the crescent moon above the palmetto tree.

It should of been me,
but, it is his heart that beats to the heat of the south.
It is his spirit tattooed, branded and pigmented by piedmont red clay.
It is his brown hands raised in celebration of the block and the flock
        he flies with.

When it is cold, we all turn south.
When it is cold, we all turn south.

I wilted sickly and indifferent under the South Carolina sun.
Jeffery always understood the heat and the hood
like he was born with the taste of sweet tea on his lips
and the drawl of vowels blooming from his tongue.

He was all collard greens and yams.
I was all thank you, but no thank you, mam.
He was back roads and natural born kin.
He took to short cuts like daddy did.
'bout could drive with his eyes closed
tell you how to get there without a map or toll owed.
Gave directions by nature or old buildings long past.

He say, *when you get to that big tree, that forks the road*
bear right then, when you get to where the Sears building usta be
you know you just 'bout there.
That's how it was for him in the hood,
knowing his way around,
knowing people by heart,
calling people by nicknames:
Chopper, Pumpkin and Cuda Boot
and then try to make you know' em
just like my daddy did.
Glenis, you Know Chris and 'nem
live at the top of the screet
You know his Momma 'nem.
Jeffery has a road map of the hood
in his veins pumpin' Highway 25
from his heart's compass holding true
spilling with loyalty he had for his crew
that same loyalty that carried him down roads
he should have never gone
following the flock on the block.

But, he has circled back now
spreading his wings in serious service,
growing muscles he never knew he had
flexing true power by severing some ties
that needed to end to sustain his growth
into becoming a man.

Walking out of the ocean backwards,
fed himself on knowledge, healing beats,
sweated salt and soulful rhymes,
while nestling his grandson and three kids
and extending his arms by producing other artists on the block.

Glenis Redmond

Now, they all flock to him—
little brother to me—
big man to kids on the street.
He helps them capture the cruelty and beauty of their lives in tune.

He is beating it out
He is beating it out in black in white
both gentle and sweet eyes that tell
he's always been too tender for this world.

Now, he lays his tracks down with music
with all his dues paid, he paves the way with grooves
and understands his world through song.
So if you ever long for your soul to be filled, catch the wave.

Turn yo' radio up.
Turn yo' radio up.

Better yet take a drive south
down 25 before the highway gets wide.
Stop and listen to a fierce sound
pelting over crickets and cicadas
loud and proud that's my lil' bro'
keepin' it real.
Pressing the ivories down
While holding the hood high.

a time for planting,

Z

In memory of Zora Neale Hurston, writer (1896-1961)

How do you hold a name like Zora?
How do you carry it off?
Start off with a slim chance,
bottle it deep in the middle
of a brown sassy smart slip of a girl.
Chisel a face in defiance,
frame it with a trademark black hat,
fashion her eyes until they sing of moonlight visions,
usher her into any room with her aura echoing of prayer and redemption.
Find her in the black and white photos
decked in riding pants, one leg cocked like a gun
on the running board of her car, Sassie Susie
the other,
rooted in the earth
and I don't take no mess,
I ride with the wind, the water and the trees.
If you don't know me, you better ask somebody, you better recognize.
Me, writer of ebony tongues,
keeper of found treasures and lost loves.
Me, braiding back porch talk into lore.
Me, speaking of how *Their Eyes Were Watching God*
and knowing his eyes were watching me.
Zigging a zagged line
in the southern turn of the century
out of Eatonville,
black-owned, black-run.
Find her
on the open range
because she could, on the open range
and she did, on the open range
kept going
listening to trash-talk and tales.

Kept folk alive in the word
those who died long before.
How do you hold a name like Zora?
You hold it like stars in your eyes
How do you hold it?
How do you hold her?
How do we keep hope in our eyes?
Rearrange the alphabet.
Begin with Z.

Glenis Redmond

A SIMPLE ACT

Tribute to Fannie Lou Hamer (1917 - 1977)

There is power in a simple act,
an intelligent step,
overriding the ignorance of labor to no end.
When did her deliverance take hold?
Spirit quaking
sending a wave through the whisper of the song
she sang,
we've come to know so well.
This little light of mine
I'm gonna let it shine.
On that day, what was the particular?
Was it the white-hot summer sun
or one piece of cotton
adding up to one too many on her back?
Adding fuel to a spirit
ready to jump free of the land
that tied her by slight of hand.
Was it the wisdom of God?
I believe it was
singing to her bones
humming a freedom she only dreamed but never knew.
She became a vessel full of the Holy Ghost
or ghosts of ancient sisters and brothers singing.
It is time sistah, keep the faith, rise.
She could have remained planted there,
her heart and spirit yoked like solid mounds.
Instead the burning bush came to her in the field.
Turned her into the Rock of Gibraltar, moving,
wrestling with fate in downtown doors
leading to white marbled halls—
ready to vote
take

pass any test
cross the line
Where God done signed her name.

UNCLE WALTER

Tribute for Walter Bailey

Uncle Walter was all brown suit serious
about the Lord.
A handkerchief-brow-wiping-holy-sweatin'
kind of man
Uncle Walter studied on kindness
therefore kindness studied on him.
Planting a sweet smile on his face,
blessing him with an ever ready hand
to pat our churchgoing backs.
He was all this, but mostly he was
a Praise the Lord with a Holy Ghost
Singing Stiff-legged Shuffle Dance.
And he danced
        as he sang
and he sang while he danced
calling forth the whole of Bethlehem Baptist Church
to *sing it children one more time*
and he did
and we did
three, five, seven more times.
He obeyed the Lord and so did we
whipped up in his "Praise the Lord" frenzy.
He didn't need no hymnal
the words written like God's words 'cross his chest,
memorized from his old-timey *bye and bye*,
flying out from his mouth like holy rain.
He didn't need no songbook, he was a walking hymn
and every song filled each step he took
made every soul stand up
take a listen and dance.
I say they don't make men like Uncle Walter no more
blessing us with the chorus

I want somewhere, somewhere
somewhere to lay my head,
somewhere to lay my head,
somewhere to lay my head.
We know now with blessed assurance
heaven has smiled on him
blessed him with a golden pillow
and somewhere to lay his head
and we all shout,
Hallelujah one more time!

Glenis Redmond

WITH HEART AS WELL AS HANDS

for the N.C. Center for Nonprofits

We step one hundred steps on this journey if we step one
leading to and fro beating a well-worn path leading to what must be done.
Some mornings it is hard to put one foot before the other,
but that mustard seed we call the sun continues to rise in the east
and so do we,
feeling the heartbeat of morning streaking red
carrying fine lines like a spider spinning a well done web
weaving tightly with hands as well as overflowing hearts
casting long lines like fishers upon the waters.
We are all called to this extending, reeling, releasing.
Some are called to calm and steady with gentle hands.
Some fight as well as pray
and others called to feed the poor and heal the sick,
a solid few to teach and protect the children.
Some remain unseen, firm braces upholding bridges,
and strong like oak planks holding steady our best laid plans
in and out of the chaos of the city
out into the desert ending the drought in the land.
We do not carry bucket-to-bucket sloshing.
We do not carry or hold for we are the water,
colorful bountiful hues flowing. We are
silver, bronze, indigo, ebony, pearl and golden waves
giving rise to promise where there was none,
giving rise to harbors of hope,
with the laying on of hearts as well as hands
looking to our fragile future
we step and believe in the magic of weaving
we step and believe in the spinning
we step and believe with understanding
we step knowing that it will never be easy

we may as well not see tomorrow
if we do not step and believe
in this promise of a tighter together
blending and stitching our strength as one.

Glenis Redmond

STRONG STITCH WOMAN

for Peggy Baldwin Loyd

She winds the clock gingerly with friendship,
threading love by hand,
creating by heart one-stitch-at-a-time memories —
knowing the way others have forgotten,
or never learned in this silver-quick world.
Pointing to portals found
on the quiet path labeled: *giving.*
Her treasures, generous
speak of another world,
a slow golden spinning orb,
a silent meditation soaked in sunray shedding light,
holding quilted tapestries of birds,
silk, satin, cotton, and time spent.
Her gifts shine
reminding others of a sparrow's wing,
a beauty without fanfare.
She does not know of her large glow
or how her hearth fire shines even in shadow
flaming everywhere she goes,
as a host of God's creatures follow her lead
trailing gracious gifts, of humbled unspoken words
symbols of the soft world
she weaves.

STEP-SISTER

for Patricia Starek

You
in your stepping,
stepped into my heart
calling out to shadow places.
You step with the brilliancy of a sun spiral called compassion.
You blaze with laughter that bursts doom into one million stars.
You step with the certainty of June offering no apologies for spring.
You step firm even when you are afraid,
when you can't find that perfect thingamajiggy from Ikea
to get your life together.
But you keep trying,
keep organizing the clutter,
trying to cease the dissension in your everyday world.
You ride hard even though you have an EZ pass.
You could not be impervious to a stone,
listening to abandoned cat cries on the streets of Harlem.
You bolt like a stallion
onto buses, cars, taxis, bikes, subways, skates and trains
arriving like no other
in any city.
The world keeps coming and you keep steppin' my friend
through tears,
through fears,
every single one.
You don't let them name you or claim you.
You step to Brooklyn, Newark and Manhattan
drawing letters in sand or whatever it takes
for children to learn how to read.
You show them how to rebuild their world
letter brick by letter brick.
Teach them to rebuild
their world on

Glenis Redmond

A, B and C.
You tell them
these letters are steps
leading everywhere you need to go.

Denizen of New York,
Citizen of Humanity ,
Poet of Fire,
and
Lover of Words,
        keep stepping
as your students
follow your lead
up and over
and right on through.

MORE THAN

for Mary Ann Jaben

More than,
a semester of lesson plans,
a steady drum calling roll,
a pair of scrutinizing eyes counting heads,
a mouth ticking for a plea of silence,
a mound of tests to be graded,
a watch keeping time of a full eight-hour day.
More than,
the grating of chalk across the board,
a landscape of children restless,
the red ink pen of correction,
the grind of grading report cards,
the pages between the book,
the acts in a play,
grammar, spelling and chapter tests.
There are exceptions to every rule,
too many to be counted
like *i* before *e* except after *c*.
The taking away
the dividing,
the abacus of the soul adding up to so much.
Like when a child takes a leap no one can see.
Not the six inches of growth in six months,
not the uncomfortable stretching of sinew,
the painful lengthening of bone,
the ripening of vocal chords.
But the leap frog of the mind unfurling to an uncharted star,
whether the spark of a remembering
or a new neural groove laid.
Sometimes a lesson is more.
Held and kept for life
In that pocket of satin red

a heart holding the lesson learned,
a boundary going beyond rules,
a wildflower growing in a field
along with the dragon and butterfly
flittering alive from a teacher's mind
traveling beyond bone,
structure and frame
lifting words
to wing from the printed page.

a time for birthing,

NECESSARY ART

dedicated to Lynn Greer

She don't make babies or mince words.
She labors paint, water and paper mixed with emotions
water coloring life mostly purple and red
blazing love with the temperament of fire.
She has gone to France to learn more about the theory of color.
Though she has learned much in her forty-two years
she has gone to Provence
for a chance to spy lavender growing in bunches and straight delicate rows.
And she will bring some back home to plant
in her garden she keeps year 'round.
She is gone to France but she will return
to the south, burning even more
with her lavender brush bleeding compassion
for the figures humbled
standing next to century-old buildings.

She is going to France as she has gone everywhere;
her heart in her brush leading directly to her veins.
Her hopes higher than the airplane she took to get there.
She has gone to perfect her craft of mothering,
not wondering how her boys or her girls will grow,
not split over going to France or to the PTA,
but her heart bleeding magentas and yellows
giving birth to babies generated from her color wheel.
Raised from paintbrush tip and regal hues
coaxed into life just to let them go.

She is not bad because she has forsaken the maternal hearth
for the sacred paintings hanging over her perpetual womb.
Her days are spent bringing wrongs to right
bandages to knees and splints to sprains,
all with a turn of the wrist,

a tilt of her head,
to capture light
letting spirit emerge
through painted people
with countless words unsaid.

Glenis Redmond

FINDING HOME

for Avery August Climo Matthews

Finding a place where
two hearts
four arms open
where you will rest
many days of your life ... spending happy hours
in a great house extending beyond bloodline,
a caring beyond bone,
a path winding along Appalachian curves
tucks and grooves.
Nestled in this beauty
sage is burnt in your honor
sacred blue corn spread
in the summer of your birth
in the hope of your name
in the belief of your newborn cries.
Libations are poured
liberating the world.
Your tears riverlink
us to our greater selves
a circle-dream of two hearts
four arms curved, grooved and tucked
leading to home, nation and world.
You are a blessed soul.
Son of Ali,
Son of Sebastian,
Citizen of the World.
I bow down
touch the ground
four times:
in beauty
in love
in truth

in belief
of this heart
and arms churning of the world.

BIRTHDAYS

They are me.
They are of me.
They are more than me.
They are two sweet sips of beauty
steeped in the language of dreams,
earth, sky, fog, clouds, and undiluted blue streams of girlish songs.
Their innocence sings of worlds I once knew.
They are my first and second born in one birth.
The first, an airy indigo guru full of wisdom and insight.
The second, a solid ginger prayer bundle
burning with the intensity of fire.
They are two but more than two.
They are my many poetic stories happening at once.
I was once a simple woman with a shallow voice, a hollow bell.
Motherhood struck the chord, brought me forward with sound,
inducted me into the tribe of poetic prayer tongue,
transformed me into a Holy Roller of words and worlds,
straddled me across the abyss of pain and joy,
marinated me in the juice of what my daughters have made me
a fierce mother eagle, a hawk, but mostly a Phoenix rising,
wingspan wide with the one true color: *compassion.*
A poet mama bird feeding herself, her babies and others with words.
So when I speak of multiple births, I am including myself.
My girl self grew from the food of woman talk
became wise from woman ways,
growing upward and round
with the power of circles,
embracing hearts, arms and hips
with the carriage of large loads:
babies, joy, and the dark root of sorrow.
On this journey to becoming mama, mom and mother,
I have traveled beyond bone.
That passage brought me back with a stretched soul,

made me wide by my only two true epic poems.
I am kept alive by their telling
and my wings flare with hope and redemption.
Showing me how in everything we do
no matter what, we touch the world.
I am a rough rock smoothed by kissing waters
raining double blessings down
with the best of
earth and sky.

POETIC FATE

My daughter represents what I am
and what I am not
inheriting the knowledge of numbers
strange strand passed down along her paternal side
her father's mother relinquishing a coded mathematical language
I never understood,
that DNA being exempt from my genes.
At age 6, Celeste explains to her sister
Algebra is easy. It is simply solving for the unknown.
In disbelief I stare, absorb the meaning.
Then the joke she shares with her father,
his house sits in the hypotenuse of a right triangle.
A what?
Celeste is offhand with this knowledge
geometrically minded
she slides right into origami simplified
a swan, a wasser baum, a box, a frog.
Me, frozen,
I stare at my child as I looked at my elementary classmates,
who computed so easily,
who understood numerical sequences.
I knew just enough to know
I was not getting it.
Call my fate fear or arrested development
in having to take mathematics for dummies
dreaded chalk board long walks to the front of the room
humiliated by the scream in my brain to self, *you are dead girl walking.*
My abacus counting free hand by my side
entering numbers as if it were the lottery
hoping upon hope
wishing upon some cosmic magic
that this time I have the winning number
hoping for a hit from my pick.

Just once I want to capture the finite
like a firefly in a summertime jar
not just by chance or a guess.
I am the subjective test queen
absolutely ruling on essay questions,
where I can wax my poetic heart out.
In the waning
I believe the point of the unknown
is better left there   alone
in that vast region.
After all, isn't that the reason poets write poems?

Glenis Redmond

TOO MUCH

She has always been too much
indigo blue or fire ant red —
a dervishing whirl of shapeshifting moods.
Celeste,
the best mess,
the untidy half of the twins,
tornado twister
sporting tangled clothes,
disheveled hair,
ever-present food or drink spills on clothes,
a lovable collection of the unlikely,
flashes of untapped Einstein genius,
glimpses of Gandhi-like spiritual brilliance,
wrapped in a young teen
holding fast to faith,
saving the world
with all the answers buried in the wreck of her room.
beneath unwashed glasses, the funk of soccer shoes,
the stench of a fermenting orange
hiding out in her book bag for six months.
She's a strange brew
of crumpled homework assignments,
botched artistic attempts,
a quirky collection of both fact and fiction.
She saves everything
for the sake of accidental science or art.
She won't let me throw anything away,
scraps of paper,
elastic from her old underwear,
box tops,
fussy odds and ends,
outgrown clothes,
a fine deal for Goodwill shoppers.

She will not sacrifice one item
in this clutch of chaotic creativity;
she is a loyal believer of art,
even in the midst of this celestial clutter.
I want to clean it up,
before I spy myself
all over her room.

Glenis Redmond

M.I.T.

(mother in training)

We called her lil' momma or baby Jeanette.
Before she could talk
she'd walk defiantly and with a purpose.
Her chubby hands closed into fist.
Her mouth set with serious adult determination.
Some children come here like that.
Emerge fully grown
with a rock solid sense of self.
Some
come here with a mission.
This one
always got a hand on her hip
or the other one pointing like an arrow
to what needs to be done
or better yet doing it herself.
This whipstitch of a happening,
Amber, my youngest,
rock solid as her name.
I didn't make her this way,
she came like this on her own.
Knowing what is what
every which way and that,
and pitching in at just the right time.
She's got cabinets to clean.
She's got beds to make.
She's got TV channels to change.
We call her R. C. Q.
for Remote Control Queen.
She's got her finger on the pulse.
She's got a sister to keep
and she even tries to run me with,
Mom a tattoo is totally out of the question.

What will it look like on you when you are eighty?
I let loose with a look that says this is my body and my money.
She deflects my words
with rolling eyes and an all-knowing sigh.
She's got maternal instincts vibrating way too high.
What can I say?
It comes from my side.
She is just like me
even more than I ever was.
She's got a schedule posted on her wall,
wake up 6 a.m., 6:30 a.m. wake up rest of household.
Some children come knowing what must be done,
carving the way carrying on.

Glenis Redmond

a time for uprooting,

THE UNBEARABLE HEAT
OF SOUTH CAROLINA

for Langston Hughes

When I get to be a poet
I am going to pen poems
about the unbearable heat of South Carolina
and I am gonna put the color of the Carolina sky in it,
that perfect tint of springtime blue
wafting the perfume breeze of the yellow Jasmine,
calling to the Carolina Wren to rise.
And I am going to put the frilly froof of the Mimosa in it
and thick generous Magnolia blooms
and the magenta of the Crepe Myrtle
trying to reach its twisted sister,
lavender Wisteria turning on its vine.
And I will talk of cotton,
corn and tobacco, too.
But mostly cotton.
And of those crooked tree trunk fingers
that picked the fabric of our lives
and how those large plantation foundations
were laid firm on humped and curved backs.
And I will put some gospel songs in it,
laced with the fire of West African chants,
singing of how these haunted beauties
dwarfed the shotgun shacks
next to sharecropped fields and factory mills.
And I will write down the chain
of broken black white people making a living on prayers—
Whispering the words, *get by anyway you can.*
And I will stand next to this quiet Palmetto faith
and understand the thunderstorms of the past grounded in red clay.
And I will release my own prayers of gravity
and hold tight to the belief

they will rise like the morning sun
and the nighttime crescent moon.
I will stand fast to the faith that carries my pen across blank pages
and I will sweat strong sweltering lines
of both celebration and woe
when I get to be a poet
and pen poems
of the unbearable heat of South Carolina.

Glenis Redmond

CROWS

I hear crows everywhere I go.
Black beaks and wings find me everywhere
speaking of shadow acts and sorrow.
They have Ogun's ebony eyes
and Oshun's silver breath.
How long can a person live not knowing their soul?
Who can say the exact moment we were infected by our own garnet fever?
A jewel infection leading us to take brave steps
to our own annihilation
leading to rebirth.
When the crows first spoke,
I did not recognize it as resuscitation.
I believed they were mocking me.
I pleaded with them to speak in a language my mind could swallow,
to give me a sign I could read.
The brilliant red of a stop sign,
the all too familiar crisscross
of a railroad X,
these I know.
Here in this after, I still do not speak crow.
Yet my prayers are answered all the same.
I comprehend my soul's tongue and the duty
of these black wings brazen as a neon sign.
Their ebony presence in the air does not spell doom
neither does it stream like steel bodies
turning towers into ash and people into smoke.
These congregations of black birds are loud witnesses
wailing like the soulful mourners at Mt. Zion Baptist Church.
They do not exact death.
They scream it
carry it
pall bearing what we humans
wreak in God's holy name.
I say again,
I hear the crows everywhere I go.

A SLAVE NAMED PATIENCE

This must be how irony swims,
an insatiable mouth, wide with suckling.
I am pulled to it every time,
to these ungrounded stories.
The timeless wonder within me
opens to the unacknowledged wind,
these lives wanting release through my bones.
A slave named Patience bears too much pain
for any one body to live or hold,
an unlikely load of both tragedy and beauty,
sisters conjoined at the chest wrapped hand in hand
pulling from earth, sky and the ethers in between.
These elements melt me to knee-bent prayers,
but these sisters echoing pain and quiet beauty
stand me up, walk me right through the cemetery gate.
Pain takes the greatest hold, while I scream questions.
Beauty fastens me to hope with the flare of her magenta dress.
She tells me to record everything, the good along with the bad.
Write it all down. How can beauty speak to this life? Patience's that is.
But beauty don't pay me no mind
she still comes around my house, always unannounced,
settles herself down like the colors of a sunset horizon
embedding its jeweled self across my treasure chest.
My heart still flowers,
that sickle cell anemic bloom of despair
of this buried life scrawled in a two hundred year old brick
P A T I E N C E
her name sticks like an eight-letter thick soup in my throat
wreaking daybreak beneath my bones.
Her lot catches me hot as a newborn
feverishly alive among the dead.
It is true I never saw her,
PATIENCE that is.

Glenis Redmond

I will never know if her dress smelled of smoke or rain,
if her face was lined with a tree-like mahogany,
or if her eyes were sacrificed to a milky blue.
My fear lies across the wrong side of Jordan
fading away like the earthly always does.
But Patience, she never fades
never loses her glory.
She just keeps coming
keeps calling out my name
down that long southern road
or through swirled sips of afternoon tea.
She keeps calling me to take her up
and carry her
with her bags packed,
a large load
or is she willing
to carry me
taking me up under this brilliant, horrific roof of sky?

BURYING THE DEAD

Memorial for slave cemetery in Asheville, N.C.

In our town
out of sight
past Wyoming Street
up on the hill behind St. John's Baptist Church
lay aged bricks, rocks and baskets of bones,
where the dead are not truly dead,
their silent mouths far from quiet.
Speaking crow they wrestle the blueness from night
and lift sorrow from its deeply veiled sleep.
Through Kenilworth
runs an Indian trail,
a forested hill
I could call my own.
I don't.
Not too far from downtown
living beneath the tangled brush
a cemetery of slaves merge with the Cherokee and their trail
unmarked lines carrying both streams of blood
that course unceasingly through my veins.
Both trails have found my heart
intersecting where spirit meets bone
and I have taken to walking the block
putting down feet and prayer
on both foreign and familiar ground.
On this walk I am found,
joined, graced and haunted
by an urgent need quite like death and birth.
Call it a bitter dream I keep reliving
try to pin it on the past
remind myself of the passage,
the dead will bury their own
they haven't so the crow flies,

Glenis Redmond

pecks and caws on my forgetfulness
calls to me through shutters tilted open.
I rise from my couch of restless sleep.
I rise from my doing
from the mundane task of washing clothes.
I rise because I cannot wash my hands of this
these spirit bodies hovering
souls littered across the land
calling to open skies,
open hearts,
any vessel open
as to how they have not rested in life or death;
how they have not claimed this land
or purchased a stone to mark
their passing.
Lost
on a hill
behind a church
in a town
in these mountains.
This cry is not made of "i"
it is made of a glorious tormented collective
of a blueblack and red "we."
Spirits torn
into a cry so bitterly ruined
of broken wings, cracked bones and splintered dreams.
Screaming the woes of heavy air
and the pain it takes to turn gospel into blues;
a weight only crows can carry
on their blueblack backs
singing the harsh call to be heard
the call of crows
chanting through unpleasant beaks

the unsingable to us,
we who are on earth walking
are indeed
the dead
in need
of waking.

Glenis Redmond

DISLOCATED HEART

No cast, splint or sling hastens the healing of a heart.
It just keeps on pumping
playing the same ole' broken hearted memories.
Keeps playing how it all went down so badly.
No past act is left unturned
so the heart takes a stand and leaves the room
seeks another home,
where nothing moves.
Freedom is left to wildflowers growing strong in a July field.
I don't attend to my heart anymore,
this cold gray stone perched on pillars.
It could be alive with its placid look;
no one would ever know
how it searches with such a weak pulse
like a ruined bitter stream green with muck
muscles weak with shame
seeking a clearwater quiet place to live
recalling the thirst of how it used to beat fierce
like a wild thing blind to fear.

a time to refrain from embracing,

WHITE FLIGHT

You sing sweet lullabies.
You talk soft singing folk.
I should have known
it would end like this
quiet and mostly off-key,
with you saying to me
I need to keep it light.
That's white, right?
Or was my heart
just a place to visit,
on the wrongsided track?
You had no business
stepping to my door.
Did you have a clue?
keeping it light
is a luxury
this black girl
cannot afford.

LEAVE ME BE

leave me 'lone
leave me be
leave me sleeping on a couch
leave me waiting in a room
wondering what the fuck was that
wondering who the fuck are u

Glenis Redmond

I WAS VIRGINAL

I was virginal
when we met
the color i wore,
white
a true reflection
of goddess.

I was virginal
forget the eleven years of marriage
the scars up along
this skin case of mine
the caverns of stretched skin
from a twin birth,
the disaster of my spirit
left from a miscarriage two winters ago
the dreams deferred
the love adrift
the scars of passion
the karmic debt
the back bent
over crosses carried
from thirty-four years of living a black woman's life
Don't mistake my age
as an admission of guilt
You haven't read one
page in this book
You checked it out
just the same
plucked it from the shelf
perused the cover
the only thing
you understood
was my name

As you kissed
this violated frame
licked my swollen fruit
as it hung lusciously low
mistaking it for meat
to be slaughtered
eaten
yet not honored
the dress I wore
was not red
That was the fresh color of wine
I drank in the temple
with Jezebel
my sistah
virginal too
her mission scripted
just like mine
Where were you when
I spoke in tongues?
Did you need an interpreter's ear?
I will repeat lest you do not overstand
I was virginal
I was virginal
I was virginal on my way to Zion
progressing barefoot up that hill
I was singing Yahweh's praises
I was seeking a promise land
I mistook you for the hint of that shore
and now I am bearing broken glass
You pursued me with fervor
and the fever of a dervish
spinning out of control
I met you willingly

made the detour
as kundalinis rose
suspended
to untouched heavens
I recognize
how we both look like Jesus
or was that fear or hate
in your eyes
when we lifted to the skies?
You had to see
you had to hear
as you came
as you saw
as you conquered.
You had to view
the crucifixion, the resurrection,
the uncovered shame,
the blood splattered,
the scars with no names.
I was looking for black harbor,
dark haven,
a protected place to land.
I thought it was you,
I, virginal, but also the fool
dangling on your cliff's edge
devoured and skewered
by your priceless chaotic spear.
You are done,
but I am not dead.
I am lifting my head.
I am unfurling the kink in my spine.
I am turning the cosmic corner.
I am hovering close to moonlight.

Getting perspective from the height.
You see me burning uncontrollably bright.
Shrink back to your recesses.
You will know me from way back when
five thousand years ago.
You, Mayan Prince, this here ain't no game.
You remember too.
How I had been slaughtered
on the mountainside in Peru.
Offered in your father's name as a burnt sacrifice
this stench
is not incense
this stench
is not sage
this stench
is fire
this stench
is me
this stench
is my flesh
this stench
is my name in smoke across the sky.
I rage virginal
virginal
virginal
My God, virginal.
What were you?

Glenis Redmond

SONG OF DISRESPECT

It was the hair
the golden waves of hair,
the wavy waterfall length of it
or maybe the voice,
the jagged tone falling down like rough rain
or his hands, his no nonsense hands
pummeling iron, wood and wax
into shapes under his control.
Or, it could have been the power of the unknown.
The romance of mystery.
It gets me every single time.
We never really talked
listening to large-eyed silences.
Felt the thick tensioned pulse from our trembling skin
leading us to touch after three weeks of quiet.
He chose to use his tongue to say,
"I came just to see you at lunch and
it's me and you until the break of dawn."
Obviously he was just sampling a Seventies song.
I say, "I never believe what 'they' say."
He says, "Believe everything."
I don't, but hope a little anyway.
This is the sad condition of my crazy heart, *hoping a little*.
Dawn came,
so did he
just not with me.

a time for tears,

CONTRITION

Grief stands closest to me
in a crowded room.
Along a chalk line of alone
I draw around myself to keep me going
reeling from death.

I land in a corner
drawn to a ray of light calling me out.
I want to touch this round pearl bleating
to soothe the pit of my empty bowl.
Is this my father calling for forgiveness?
Or is this heavy teardrop the metronome
of my own laden step,
glowing,
a sliver of moon of my own regret
begging to be let go?

SACRUM

The doctor says, *disc deterioration.*
In other words, *my father is losing his spine.*
My next thought is the children's song
that teaches the anatomy of bones,
the terrain of the body
the thighbone connected to the hipbone
the hipbone connected to the backbone
the backbone connected to the....
My next thought quiets my singing in one solid knowing moment,
I realize *my father has been losing his spine a little all along.*
If this poem were about forgiveness,
if I knew where his pain began,
I would take my index finger
trace it along that beginning of the Ivory Coast.
At the base of his head, the Medulla Oblongata
I would sing it into being on that Virginia Plantation.
Along the Thoracic vertebrae
I would call him out of that slavery,
release the yokes and chains of his sharecropper past.
I would chant Cherokee,
Sioux
and Seminole
out of the chakra of his throat.
I would follow his trail of tears
leading down the curve of his back,
the Lumbar and the Sacral regions,
and walk along flanks of cotton in his Jim Crow history.
I would stand next to him,
that malnourished man-child at the Air Force recruitment office
as he spreads the poison spiriting himself away
all with the signing of his name until he is only a misted ghost.
I would be there calling him back from all the torn places,
rattling bones,

Glenis Redmond

blowing smoke into this shadow of a shadow,
balancing the forces of air too harsh
for one already prone to breaking.
Maybe just maybe this signing was his one holy act;
bench pressing the family,
and the whole of his past beyond any weight he lifted before.
Maybe this was the beginning of bones breaking.
But he picked them up anyway his shape skeletal and bare.
He configured himself into the shape of leaving,
an internal dowsing rod,
a compass pointing magnetic north,
anything leading away to take him from before.
A drought of rain is severe.
A drought of marrow is devastation.
If my weight could hold it,
I would lift him to a tender liquid light
like the others, who looked on him from his youth,
and called him *Sonny Boy*.
He, a good looking slender man with hope in his eyes.
I'd spy that slim child placing his polished boot upon promise.
I would pour into him his calcium-spent self where ivory keys
            could not fortify.
Taking him down dark alleys into the pool-shark dens
no matter how many gigs played and clubs inhabited.
The spirit knows bones feed on calcium and light.
Tender fingers slid over keys eventually leading to bars,
leading to his favorite amber liquids of Jack Daniels and Jim Beam.
Maybe he tried to be present both there and here.
Maybe the slave in him revolted,
the Indian in him rose up,
the pianist within him began to play tunes.
But he is sitting now
sitting with the weight of all that soldiering,

he believed to be a pocket guide for better living.
Marching him through straight rows of cotton
corn
tobacco
into pouring stiff drinks of Old Grand-Dad,
Crown Royal and handed him a case of Black Label.
Taught him to raise hell all night,
as long as he was straight and squared away in formation
by 0600 that morning.
Our nights and weekends, *his* second job.
Our house on alert with the Sergeant in him in command,
and the liquid amber out of control.
He patrolled the halls of our lives on midnight shifts
cloaked with the wrath of Jack and two types of Jim.
With battle fatigue we addressed the casualties of war.
A son visibly wounded in the fight,
wearing scars to school like a uniform no second grader
        should have to bear.
The teacher reports to the base commander,
the base commander barks orders
"study war no more in the home
or be dishonorably discharged."

What they caught and taught they didn't treat.
Fist turned instead into verbal missiles
launching into our deepest centers.
Yet we carried on like soldiers on a tour of duty
with a sense of purpose,
standard operating procedure.
Survival our greatest mission.
We were hemmed in by heavy-handed creases,
lost in the spit-shine of shoes and high polished brass,
living between the stiff finger salute,

Glenis Redmond

standing at attention for inspection.
Our straight backs gave way to gradual wear and tear
of never being at ease.
Our familial bones breaking,
a slow de-ossification.
If this poem were about forgiveness,
our foundation would begin to mend
where it never took hold;
our sergeant in charge leading the way,
a crooked man walking with wings.

SURELY NOT MY BROTHER

"You ain't nobody, never will be," he screams.
This is how I know he is slipping into the crack.
It is in the timbre of his voice,
the quake of the house,
it is in the tremble in the ground.
This is how I know he is never coming back.

He has slayed me
with one thin sliver of who he once was.
I am fresh fish sliced
with the vengeance of who he is now.
Who is this? Cane?
Menacing me with below the belt words
wounding me with the gun of my father.
Surely not my brother.
The one who had the lighthouse look in his eyes.
The one who came from the same familial fate as I.
The one who traveled through the same amiable womb
no solid foundation
teetering on doom.
Surely not my brother.
Now he has found his rock and it rules!
Rules out allegiance to brotherly sisterly love.
Rules out the pact of like minds and artist heart.
Rule out the "*I got yo' back no matter what.*"
I know the world has cracked and he has slid.
When I hear the timber
and the rattle in the skies,
"Forget You!
What I got you need."
There is no more, "*I love you.*"
He has flipped the script
and he has been slipping since the day he was born.

Bright-eyed boy
broken from the breast by male hands
with the belief, "*You shouldn't be held too long.*"
He wants to suck.
Now he is caught in the crack of serious need.
He is renting when he could buy.
He is selling out when he could live in the home of his own soul.
I could tell you he is drowning
but he is already dead.
Spirit siphoned and hocked for each rock.
Surely not my brother.
Slipping out, sipping out, tripping out
pied piping, taking his children
my children,
anybody's children as he goes down.
Surely not my brother.
For he could have died back in '74
hit flat by a Fiat against a stone wall;
He was spared for this?
To chuck rocks into the abyss?
To live in perceived bliss?
I can't believe this.
See for my baby bro there ought to be angels in tow
raining kisses from a 4th of July sky
an Emancipation Proclamation to free my baby brother's soul.
He can't swim.
I can, but only enough to avoid the rocks in the undertow.

But I, a poet,
never had nothin'
but these few words.
I want to break over you,
in eulogy and christen you,

and rock you,
in your aquamarine cobalt coat of dreams.
I, your sister
I want to rock
you awake.

LONELY GIRL

She's got lonely wrapped up in her eyes.
One blink and she travels backward into those onyx jewels.
She's gone,
a little girl outdoors
with her feet tucked in house shoes,
draped in morning drag
sleep dangling in each step
with pillow marks across her soul.
She's not slow.
Just prefers to moonwalk up on the ceiling,
or on a planet with twelve moons
or any super-powered place
that gives her superhuman strength.
So she can make it, and take it one more day.
Anywhere from this in between she's living.
Her vacation is a gaze out of any open window.
If you don't know her,
you will spy her dressed
in the childhood she never lived.
Disney secured hanging from each ear
draped around her neck and wrists
blazoned in bold red and blue across her chest.
She is keeping it light any way she can
flashing a Mickey Mouse beacon
that shouts, *I am still just a kid.*
But, she is wearing that old look in her eye.
She has witnessed too much before her time.
Taking on the mother load
her recesses perpetually sacrificed.
Roller coaster rides exchanged for daily ghetto dramas.
She has taken what has been handed down to her
a generation of pain, dimming black jewels.
Her inheritance is carried in the strain of her hands

and carried on the bulk of her back
and that dull gleam of sleep in her eyes
while she cooks at nine,
launders and baby-sits,
quakes you with the riddle in her eyes,
a subconscious confession
never leaving her lips.
She is paying the debt.
Clumps of jet-black hair fall
leaving bald patches,
giving way to stomachaches
skin gathering into hives.
We say too little to those who've seen too much.
She is all of our nightmares dreamed.
She is sadness personified.
Her eyes stare you in the face
take you to a place
where she is straddling fate
one foot behind grace
and the other headed over the tombstone.
Hand her
her childhood back.
But, there is no way to childhood from here.
She is busy now, growing a child of her own.
Pain begat Sorrow,
begat Regret,
begat Weariness.
Rest yo' tired head child
sometimes we all just need to rest.

Glenis Redmond

a time for embracing,

COFFEE BLACK

for Nina Simone

I love Nina Simone 'cause
she's black like me.
No cream.
No sugar
just a serious ebony swirl,
a dark and lovely sistah
singing stories of the rough road
holding all
the difficult and the comely.

I DIDN'T HAVE MY COLORS DONE

When I was a girl
I wore a faded dress of mint green
donned an uneven ebony Afro
danced to Motown
sang the blues off key

uncomely by the beige standards
of beauty in this world
I let those fair lines
not stop me

I danced
sang
until it registered.
deep in my soul
Nappiness=Happiness
power to your own blood
makes one
colorfully
whole.

Glenis Redmond

MANGO

for Tiger

I like to know where I AM
at all times.
Where I am going,
E. T. A., weather conditions, what's going on.
Contribute it to my astrology
the particular hour of my birth
my sun sign, Virgo, with Saturn in the seventh house.
I feel things strongly, deeply, passionately,
but only after careful thought and thoughtful analysis.
I've heard this refrain all too often in my life
echoed from my lover's lips,
"You think too much."
Then I disappear into his eyes.
This Rasta man, dreads falling down his back like black rain.
The way this man moves
I want to be caught in his groove and I AM.
I can't get out of the slant of his Portuguese eyes,
the firmness of his African hips.
The way that this man dips,
I want to stand up on the mountain and shout about it
thank God about it.
No, thank Jah about it.
I want to give praise
for the particular curves of this man's bones.
He is deep.
He is deep not with words.
He is deep with his two thousand year-old heart.
With his arms he has carried me to a place
where I can forget my complex make up.
He has carried me where
water washes away reason.
He has reshaped my landscape.

Made me melt with the heat of his desire.
His hands
His hands
How have they have learned their lesson?
I'd rather not know.
But I am thankful for he is all beauty and danger
the product   fire.
He looks up from that deep place in his eyes and says…
"I want to make you something to eat."
He disappears into his world.
He slowly turns inhales a mango
his world is all flesh and juice sliding between lips
as dark as magenta sunrise.
I,
do not want for naught.
I,
do not envy mango or any other foreign fruit.
I am wide open with desire,
body tight with tension
and the knowledge
I,
will become a mango
this night,
and nothing else
will exist
in his world.

Glenis Redmond

POEM KISS

for D.B.

Your kisses read like poems
your poems feel like kisses
and I can't get enough of poems or kisses
especially that tongue haiku
planted in perfect time
upon my breast
kisses falling from your lips
like amulets of much needed rain
on my thirsty desert floor
I am wet with fire
branded by tattooed kisses.

how can I sustain
a minute,
a day,
or two weeks waiting
for a poem,
a kiss,
the mark of your tongue
leaving a sweet trail of you?

I am a book opened to this chapter of you.
My skin is ink fresh wanting more.

a time for mourning,

TRAIN

Picture a fifth-grade class,
a bustling single file line
swarming with the promise of recess.
See a girl happiest away from home,
flitting more eagerly than most
about fifteen minutes of freedom.
See the smile fly from her face,
when she hears from a boy
three kids back
calls her a nigger.
See joy stop spinning on its axis.
See the trigger set off the train,
the hard slap of her hand
against his face
protecting the dignity of her race.
His cheeks redden with shock and humiliation.
Feel the slap hitting her harder the next day,
when she hears the news
of the boy who will never stand
in their school line again.
Understand the hardest blow.
Him running through the rain,
his head cloaked with jacket,
hit by a bus
he never saw coming.

PASSAGES

Mom and I talk about our familial jaunts
She says, *We were in Michigan.*
I am cheeky, I take a swing, name our family's military trek
Smugly rattling off what she already knows as if she was not along
       for the ride,
We lived in Texas, New York, France, Morocco, Spain, South Carolina,
Italy, New Jersey and right back home to South Carolina again.
We were never stationed in Michigan Mom, I say trying to jolt her
       back into this life.
We were in Michigan.
She slaps back.
Michigan, your dad and I were stationed in Michigan in 1959.
The earth begins to quake and she unravels the sky.
I sit and listen.
She begins with sorrow, a rare storm,
I was pregnant with another child then.
Her voice is a clap of thunder as she brings her stillbirth back to life.
Instinctively I midwife, hands ready with catching.
Air stilled with the glow before lightning strikes.
She drops her forty-four year old heavy load
and lets it rain ...
Your father and I left Austin, Texas.
We had orders to Oscoda, Michigan.
We drove 24 hours to arrive at the base worn out tired
to be told to go back to Detroit and rent a hotel
no one will rent to you here.
Only to arrive back at the base
the next day papers out held for a transfer to another state.
The officer says, *I don't know why the military sent you and your*
       family here
no one in this town would give you a house.

My parents leave
travel across half of America
uneasy as volcanoes
to arrive in Niagara Falls
one child less another lesson wiser.

Forty years later
My daughter Celeste and I,
travel through Michigan, too.
My uneasiness mounts
as we speed along I-40
west to Knoxville
then north on I -75
to forever.

Celeste and I spy abandoned cars.
We see the road smeared
from the blood of road kill.
Oscoda is the point we pass.
As Sojourner's children
thin ghosts do not flag us down, stop us.
Doubt gone it doesn't whisper another solitary word
on our passported mission.
We drive collecting on a debt
forty-four years past due.
Our passage bought and paid
from the sweat of black, brown and red backs.
Heirs to these crows
we on thick wings fly
with fire in our eyes
announcing the railroad
is no longer running underground
our tank filled with that burning.

Glenis Redmond

FLATLANDS: LUBBOCK, TEXAS 1986

Never trust dry hot flatland.
Never trust a land
with no trees
especially in 104 degree heat.
Summer 1986 and I was walking
>>to my graduate class and a pickup truck armed with a gun rack
>>and confederate flag centered on the front bumper flies past
>>hurls the word

>>>>>nigger
>>>>>like it were a rock.
It is more than hot in Texas and I am a long way from home
>>but not that far I think.
>>South Carolina and Texas are as close as a stone's throw,
>>when it comes to the word

>>>>>>>nigger
>>>>>>>being thrown.

I'll never forget at Erskine College, my alma mater
>>not my daddy's
>>or my daddy's daddy,
>>but mine.
I was next to rappel out the window
down the red brick tower for ROTC credit.
Richard, the lead cadet, the one who holds our trust
and the thick braided rope yells to the person on belay,

>>>>>>>"boy you as slow as a
>>>>>>>nigger."

He flinches when he finds me at his back.
I wince, for many reasons,
I wince because the word still stings,
because I know Richard is only ashamed of being caught,

Glenis Redmond

this taught
by his daddy
and his daddy's daddy.
But mostly I wince because, I know
     I am far from home, but not so far.

I continue placing one determined foot before the other
on this dry crusty shadeless walk and welcome the air conditioner
     whirring in the 410 Counseling class.
     Sitting in relief from the heat in a circle with my
        soon to be counseling peers
     only to hear one PhD candidate say,
     "You know I never saw black people as really human."

I didn't run.
I didn't throw a rock back.
I didn't push Richard out the window.
I did not try to deliver anyone from ignorance.
It is not my job.

     My job is to keep walking
        and to keep stepping on this dried cracked earth
        knowing in the stepping there is higher ground
        understanding sunlight burning
        on flatlands with no trees
        is inevitably lethal.

Glenis Redmond

READ THE SIGNS

Those roads bear names for the greats,
Martin, Malcolm and Adam Clayton Powell.
Those roads holding up Douglass, Carver and Mary McLeod Bethune,
Booker T., Arthur Ashe, and Rosa Parks.
My pen leads me down country roads,
to upstate New York,
around Fort Green, out to Long Island,
out west to California city streets,
across fields where migrant workers pick fruit by hand,
across the Atlantic to where London loops,
over to working class Liverpool scrawl,
crisscrossing the ocean connecting bridges
from Jacksonville and Louisiana Bayous,
to canyons of Santa Fe and Taos,
to Philadelphia, the city of brotherly love,
to Sandburg's city of the big shoulders.
These roads bear names of greats
but, read the signs the real signs.
Signs riddled as a cell sickled with anemia.
These cities and towns don't chant *we have overcome*
these roads sing the song of the neglected
moaning like Mahalia.
Buildings teetering on their last asbestos breath.
Jim Crow might be gone,
but his first cousin masquerades as devastation.
Schools stand like disfigured giants
their windows graced with bars
shrouding already clouded windows.
Look for a visible place of entry
and you won't find a welcome mat or any simple archway
just a greeting of metal detectors and interrogation.
This is where our children learn.
This is where they spend six hours,

five days a week,
this is where we loose them
to expand their minds
locking them down
to keep them from cutting up.
Recess is a woolly mammoth, extinct.
A field trip is a white albino alligator
exists but rarely seen.
This how we teach our children
labeling narrow roads for great women and men.
This how we have overcome.
The signs speak of cockroach laden schools
dead-ending in a third grade class,
where children breathe Langston's, A *Dream Deferred*.
As we analyze it,
one bright, wide-eyed brown girl stands little
looming large
literally asking the questions asking,
What do you do if you have no hope
if your dream is that raisin in the sun?
Her despair is way older than her nine years.
Her question as urgent as starving eyes asking for food.
At this age she should be speculating
over new jump rope chants.
Instead, she is looking for me to dispense hope
like a bubble-gum machine
or assurance, like a life jacket, a raft, a hand to pull her up.
Or, to make a dollar out of fifteen cents.
I come from bad,
she comes from worse
and though I know how to make a little change
go a long way
poetry has never seemed so small

Glenis Redmond

and a forty-five minute workshop
is the only currency I own, a small escape map,
of how I have extended my arms
around a family of my own creation.
How I caught hold to *Maya, Nikki, Alice,*
Rosa, Fannie Lou, Zora, Gwendolyn,
on to Martin, Malcolm, Adam, Carver, Fredrick,
Booker T., Arthur, Harriet, and Sojourner.
I leave her school, like I left so many others
sucked under but not giving over.
I leave offerings like prayers to God and to my ancestors
outside, outback, under an oak, maple or sometimes a pathetic bush.
Pour libations honoring the road
that she and so many are destined to travel.
These rituals and poetry are small seeds of golden faith
planted in the rubble of these public third world places
etched and outlined in neglect,
where food, books and tools are luxuries,
where doors do not grace their bathroom stalls,
much less the simple dignity of soap and water
to wash their young impressionable hands.
With pen in hand I pass it,
the power of words,
the weaving of words into worlds.
The picture of hope is anybody that has made it out
by going through.
The picture of hope is those who hold their shaking hands
teaching them to script names of heroes and sheroes
like a grandmother's poultice
across their hearts,
to bolster, build, and restore.
Read the Signs.
The children —

Glenis Redmond

they are our buildings, our futuristic foundations.
If we keep them up
not take away from their beauty glowing
plaster their bold blooms across each and every entry way
magnify their joy onto murals in bright primary colors down the halls,
we might make it to a land of holding promise.
Let them read the signs
We Care
and let us show this love everywhere,
where they live,
the street they live on,
leading from the block, to the city, through the state,
out to the nation and onto the wide world beyond,
teaching them to ride these roads
with all they have into a more brilliant future
not forgetting where they came from
and never afraid of dying in a driveby
neglecting the signs
in a place called home.

a time for love,

SALUTE TO MIRACLES

You will not hear fall from my lips the words,
there is no such work as a miracle.
I have seen Lazarus rise from the dead
time and time again.
Just when I thought this life over,
I've seen wonders right above my head.
Even when my focal point has waned,
I have viewed angels.
Even at my greatest contempt for man and myself,
I have been humbled by a quiet deed done unto me
with no regard for race or compensation.
I will neither give over my hope nor lay it down
before the shining eyes of the youth.
I will lift it up in God's name
for this is my legacy the only thing I bequeath.
There are days I would rather die with my ineptness
of not knowing how this world fits together mathematically.
Yet time and time again I have been asked to rise
to learn another lesson,
with the mouth of the Almighty
whispering into the conch of my ear,
I am not finished with you yet.
I am supposed to be alive.
I am destined to this life of fire.
I will not dismiss my life to shame or fear
I will wear my coat of Glenis
graced with an amulet of love around my neck.
I stand in life with lines
deep as pockets in my brow
showing my struggle and how this has not been an easy life.
I am the granddaughter of a sharecropper
I continue to sing my family's song
that evolved way before the cotton fields.

If you know the tune, I beg you to sing along.
I have been emancipated by miracles,
learning from the simple people in my life
to be earnest and yearning,
open to beauty.
There are days that I would rather fold my petals and die
but in knowing I understand
I would just spring forth into another day such as this.
I will either flower or wilt beneath this sun.
I will not spend my day
asking permission.
I will toil in celebratory praise
doing what growing things do.

Glenis Redmond

LOVE WAITS

Love waits
out in the night
underneath the full face of the moon
beneath the fingers of the stars extending light.

Love waits
it doesn't run through the brush
of the day-to-day jungle of traffic and gossip.
Caught up in the "*Did you know she?*"

Love waits
'til you are off the cell phone,
disconnected from the internet totally alone
away from any type of hype or trip attempting to tie you
up in that played out inner dialogue of,
"*Will they return my call or my affection?*"
Love just don't have you flippin' and trippin' like that.
Love waits I say.
Love does not endorse your multiple breakdowns, panic attacks,
or any other earthly dramas 'cause love won't play you
like a three dollar bill having you spending your heart
so when you get up to the cash register
there is no *cha-ching,* that shit is fake
it ain't even real.
Love will not play you like that.
And if some joker does,
Love waits.
Waits for you to pick yourself up
piece yourself together
with a glue labeled dignity and grace.
Love waits for you to address all your wounds with soul-aids.
They cover a lot and won't even cost you a dollar.
Remember prayer, meditation and affirmation.

"*I am a Beautiful Child of God.*"
Say it ten times every day, and when the stress is off the hook, thirty.
Remember you can dress your self up in Vera Wang
or suit yourself down in Armani.
Because it never hurts to look good but really and truly I say to you,
love is not into appearances, no matter what the ads say.
Love waits.
It is never sold out
it is always right on time.
You have all the currency you need for love
it isn't so expensive that you would have to lay it away.
Love is always in synch and never goes out of style.
You do not have to join the army, fight,
get decked out in camouflage fatigues.
There is no need to arm yourself or draw battle lines.
You do not have to fight the good fight
with love there is no need for war.
You do not need a compass or to purchase a Range Rover to get there.
You do not need an M23 Rocket Launcher or any other heat seeking
     missile device to track it down.
Love is the highest technology you will ever know, or own.
You do not have to enroll in a college course, get a Masters or PhD.
All you have to do is look in the mirror and glow.
Love waits there for you to breathe
move to the center meadow
with green pastures
with the still, still waters
look there in the water
It is Love
silver and perfectly whole
in the center of you
a blessed circle, an "*OM.*"

Love waits there still
quietly calling for you
to come back
home.

COURAGE AS A MUSCLE

Commemorating Helpmate's 25th Year

When even the clouds shout,
why don't she leave,
pack what she got left,
don't walk
run towards freedom?
When even her toddling children know
the storm in the house
looms larger than the whole gray sky outside.
The song from the chorus,
the song from the sensible says,
why don't she sprout wings instantaneously? Fly?
These people looking with earthly eyes
can't see her wings,
clipped, broken, battered.
Ruined in the very act
meant to bring her Love.
We with the big questions,
we with even bigger answers,
we with our feet planted firmly
in our freedom, shake our heads say,
all she got to do is leave.
How soon we forget.
Refuse to remember days
when we were overwhelmed
with weakness,
days ending with our fetal selves curled under sheets.
We are too past that,
we don't want
to confess we were born wet
with trembling from God's lips.
We can't remember courage as a muscle
coming over time, around time

through time, creating its own division of night and day
      to merge with us.
Not mountain, pacific, central or eastern
not governed by Greenwich
or any other town.
Courage takes its own sweet time
steeps itself in the practice
of building the heart.
Courage begins in increments,
like the first steps of a long journey.
I
have been told
first steps,
don't begin with feet,
but with unseen intentions sprouting
quiet conversations of the heart.
Some days she talks to a friend,
the next day she forgets,
regrets the promise to leave,
stays in the clutch of misery's blue-black arms.
Then, one day courage
speaks a tongue she understands,
whispers a silver prayer into her spine,
stirs her to lift the veil
make a phone call
which links her to a haven
offering twenty-five years
of a way out.
These wise hands of hope encourage her
to remove the shades,
hiding shamed eyes.
In the respite of shelter,
she cradles her own shattered jaw

Glenis Redmond

dares to cry, eventually laugh again,
to be bathed in the golden friendship
of others crowned with courage.
She shakes her frame free
rising from bent knees.
Her heart finding courage,
between the bruised moments
wakens to promises and possibilities.
Courage alive spirals a chant,
sings a benediction,
bursts open bright as a cloud
showering affirmations —
Your unconquerable spirit
incabable of being beaten.
You, sister of Lazarus,
You, miracle rising,
begin these quaking moments
stepping forward
while courage pulses in new ground.

Glenis Redmond

WHY THE Y?

for the South French Broad Branch YWCA, Asheville, NC

Because women have always come
     walking this way so long
     the right way
     on trails rough as tree bark
     but they still come with tender fingers
     kindness shining like silver moons and golden stars
     in their eyes
     tending to what must be done
     eventually stepping over boulders
     pouring themselves from separate rivers
     into a pool of reconciled sisters
     a tide easier
     blessed with women wide
     for it has always been women
     singing the nations into being,
     rocking the world upon knees,
     caressing love, this backbone of belief
     knotting golden, purple and blue threads
     holding the cloth of our dreams
     arms open embracing difficulty
     knowing the only way out
     is through
     so, we associate every day
     touching others,
     creating circles,
     including all,
     in figuring,
     in hard work ,
     lessons learned,
     from one to another
     girl to woman
     woman to girl

Glenis Redmond

to boy
to man
bronze, opal, ebony and ruby pearls
perfectly reflecting
room for all
in these halls
to stitch with heart,
to walk with soul,
to quilt with hand,
to patchwork together this human family

Glenis Redmond

PSALMS

I have held life
inside me, offered it up as two seeds
flowering into Amber and Celestial blooms.
I have received life from a gentle, pleasant sage mama,
a Buddha who speaks in black Baptist tongue love.
I have nurtured my own life growing in a way
to feed my own spiritual garden in both sweet and bitter storms.
I have a chord to this life, to all life which yokes and binds me
by blood, spirit, water and flesh
making me a mother, a sister, a cousin to life.
I do not cheat life, I do not steal life, I do not take it away.
It would suffice to say I love life in all my living.
I understand *I and I*
and the cost of carrying large loads,
the pain it takes to burst the membrane,
the blood it takes to feed nine months of the hardest labor.
Call me tenderdaughter, simplesister, womanfriend,
peaceseeker, dreamdweller, truthteller,
as long as you call me love in the end.
Join me in lighting candles,
singing circle chants,
spreading incense,
smudging earth, air and ghosts.
Come cry prayers on knees that have found the ground.
Match my lips in private, public places
talking peace whispering *no* to war.
Understand I am the daughter of an Air Force Sergeant,
who can't find the meaning in green fatigues, the battle dress of war.
Oh! hear me, I will defend my boundaries
protect my loving blooms and all those I love,
chanting Gandhi, meditating Thoreau, projecting the fire of King,
as well as Marvin Gaye's urgency of soul.
I am a loud Peaceseeker

but post-traumatic stress of past wars has left its marks on me.
I do not like war, or anything kin to it.
War does not work.
It is a broken thing, a wing
without feathers yet we still throw it in the air
with the belief this time it is going to fly.
I come from a family of the walking
with limbs incapable of flight.
I don't raise my hand to my daughters.
I have seen my fear reflected in their four year old eyes.
I made a pact that then, I will not be a party to war.
I laid down my black kettle hand and my arms used as swords.
Years of sign language had to be relearned,
but when you know better,
you do better.
I have come far having faith in little plastic time-out chairs.
It seemed such a small step and it cost me little, just my pride
and a dollar at the store.
A small step from belts, switches and backs of hands used on me.
Such a small step to another world where we war with peacetalk;
spending time understanding
why somebody got so much hate.
If there are legions more just like him to take his place
let us look this enemy in the face,
see if it bears any of our names, scars or birthmarks.
Under this one sky for life's sake,
let us walk to the green pastures leading down by the still waters,
let us find the table of our enemies laden with full hearts and open hands.
If this is the valley of the shadow of death,
if this is evil,
let us be ready to walk into it.
Because the rod and staff does comfort
as well as the bowls we call arms.

Glenis Redmond

Let us fear not this evil.
Call forth holy lines,
let them quiver with the symphony of sound
escaping like a sigh into all our nights.
Let us know that no matter what is written
no one can ever say
what war is good for
because the war song has already been played,
it shouts "absolutely nothin'".

GHETTO BOWLS

high strung, unstable, dangerous, unhinged

I am not offended by rock-hurling,
flung words are not new inventions;
I've been stoned before
for I am that unknown planet flittering
in the vast of the ebony sky
a light receding no recorded tracing
to a far off place, faraway fading.
Hope is that comet's tail
always riding away from not to,
when I attach my dreams
to a reluctant other
even if hitched to his best.
He, an unnamed star,
sinks into the abyss
like promises I made
never love hard ever again.
I slip solemn vows off my ring finger
go for what I think I know
wanting him to take me up
declare me solemnly
to claim me as his own
or fight for me
to become his lawfully
so he breathes me like need
so he never sits down on the job
always standing up.
I want him to put his hand
down or up
pull me like a stem
pluck me like a band of righteous buttercups
place me around his finger.

Glenis Redmond

Standing in all this pain
that life has dealt
has made me tired
I just want to sit with a hand to hold
to enfold, fingers to cup.
A quiet revolution of tender souls.

This is where I go when I lose myself,
the place where all shadows live.
This is how I become desperate clutching.
I am that dandelion feather never caught,
the wish blown away and received by another.
This is how I go ultimately floating
to dreams and shadows
lonely and slight
a place of hard living
difficult to swallow.
Forgetting my marriage to myself
I try to down him whole
and make him responsible for my indigestion.

It is a hard way to go flesh on asphalt
it doesn't matter though
if he doesn't look at me,
into my eyes or
if our heartbeats synchronize,
for I look past him too
trying to find my father's stare.
It is always golden at first,
then returning to dim hope.
I still run though to catch the wish in the wind
or his eyes where he finds me whole, holy,

a pleasant array of beauty of his own making.
I know, that I know not
this curious thing of father love
but I see them, daughters and fathers
all the time in crowded places holding hands
making time for a quiet love, a strong root hold
I sit in bus terminals alone
and I wonder as I wrestle with it,
with him, not out of hate but this fate
that has brought us both here
this place called ghetto where
we stand as stark naked children
in Nigeria, our bellies bloated
not knowing our place or where we came from
we stand where freedom stands and rings
we are America starving
where project walls bear graffiti across our skin
tattoos showing through all our clothes
screaming there is not enough of anything
to go around to stretch
to make a dollar out of fifteen cents
even when grace has been said
like fire from our lips
there still isn't enough for us
to pretend that we can feed ourselves
from this dim light shining
there is not enough
for our brothers, our sisters
and all our many children
yet we try to sit at this three-legged table
reconciling ourselves to the slant
that has brought us together in this way

Glenis Redmond

that has rendered us unstable
but still we pick the bowls up
even if they are empty
this is how we've been taught
having some of what goes 'round and passing it.

WE ARE NOT FINISHED YET

I haven't found a way into this poem
I am on the outside like a blind beggar with a bowl
waiting for a morsel
to help fortify my disenchanted soul.
This poem needs to be told from the inside out
but, I am given to fits of hunger
an epileptic seizure resplendent with amnesia
of how best to re-member   the heart   the head   the soul.
It has taken all of me to come to this place steadfast
and not try and escape like a black mass of crows.
I am here but I am not singing prose
I am waiting for the poem
to skim over me like holy light
and offer weight.
It is so in vogue to be indigenous people.
The truth, we are cloaked only with the dignity of our souls
but we have given in for progress and convenience an antiquity ago
So we are natives of nowhere and nothing is sacred.
We have forgotten our path and that our footprints are prayers.
The ending is here. Revelation is singing her wilted song
the night is full of blood, the clumping of hooves
and the snap of apocalyptic seals.
We inhale hope and exhale despair
holding on like desperate-eyed children
with each breath
for we realize
death has not claimed us
and we are not finished yet.
So we rise like urchins
take to the street
recover what we can
though Mozart's requiem weeps in the wind
and plays its tune in the eyes of our youth

Glenis Redmond

while we are busy helping the poor
we refuse to believe in our hearts
we are all war-torn.
In the midst of this mottled mayhem
as we enter the gates of the city
seething like a legion of lepers
while third world countries
whirl in our eyes,
showing we are haunted by the hope of our unnamed dead
and the violent poverty of their past lives.
Our sight distorted by auras
of unbelieved rape
celebrated hate
looming like that black mass of un-fed crows.
This poem is fueled and fat
with wretched neglect
but we continue to limp onward and upward still.
We are teeming with our faith
we are carried by our love
that we are not finished yet
we are not finished yet.
Though we are raw to our bones
there is nothing and no one else left
to carry this fresh regret
so we hobble down life's hollow corridor
and whisper with intent
we are not finished yet.
This chore takes more than triage
a simple labeling of things.
We must turn the sacred papers
of every holy book
touch each other like sacrament
give up apathy for Lent.

Glenis Redmond

Understand
the vowels
i and u
'til they become
u, me and we.
We do not get up from the table of our discontent
'til all the bread is broken
and fish multiplied
every hungry mouth
fed and every heart, soul
realized.
Dearly beloved,
we are all gathered today,
amen has not been said because
we are not finished yet.

Glenis Redmond

With Gratitude

I would like to thank The Divine Spirit of the Universe for giving me the wake-up call to see poetry unfurling in my life. I would also like to thank the person who gave me life, my mother, Jeneatte V. Redmond. I appreciate her thoughtful listening, understanding ways and nods of affirmative to ALL my poems. Thanks to Sandra Huie for acting as a benefactor and to Debra Roberts for being the best cheerleader ever. We run deep. A large shout out across the pond to Benjamin Zephaniah for being a poet that walks his talk and for writing "White Comedy" and also to Jackie Earley for creating the poem, "1,968 Winters" which initiated me poetically at age 11. A little later, twenty-two years later, Lucille Clifton wrote the brilliant lines, "Come celebrate with me that everyday something has tried to kill me and has failed." Her words made me literally rise from my sick bed in order to write and to live.

Thanks to Cynthia Roby for her initial comments and edits of this book. To Bob Falls of Poetry Alive! for being a great motivator and guide who insisted, "You have the performing thing down, now you have to get published." To The Vermont Studio Center for providing a magical space in which to write many of these poems. Thanks to my booking agents, John and Peggy Loyd for believing in me and having faith in my brand of Performance Poetry. Peggy thanks for the friendship and thoughtful feedback of this book. Heart and arms are extended to Patricia Starek, my "co-conspirator" who stepped with me all across the world in the name of poetry and friendship. Thanks to Robin Messing for steadfast friendship.

Thanks also to Kachina Davine for her loyal and faithful support and dedication in the office. To Heidi DuBose I extend much gratitude for her critical eye in the final phase of the book. To Lynn Greer for being a friend and working artist. Thanks for bringing my image to life with your artistic wonders. Thank you to Laura Hope Gill for being a poetic kindred sister and to Sebastian Matthews for being a writer friend and a true ambassador of the arts and to Susanne Abrams for teaching the Artist's Way and getting my poetic juices back into flow.

Sue Inman's support and mentorship in the early days was most valuable as well as EMRYS, who supported my efforts throughout the years. To Christopher Tunstall who provided a place for me to teach what I know to the many young people of Asheville through STEAM! To the Asheville Area Arts Council for providing funding for foreign travel to distant shores that always quake my soul.

Thanks to The North Carolina Arts Council for suppor ting me as a poet and teaching artist. Thanks to Amy Dumas at the Kennedy Center for the Arts. Much appreciation to the Vermont Studio Center and Atlantic Center For the Arts for providing a space to write. A big shout out for Ellen Westkaemper of the Peace Center for encouraging me to teach teachers. Thanks to M. Scott Douglass for being at the Carolina Literary Festival and making this particular dream of mine come true.

Finally to my core family my brothers Willie, Errick, Jeffery and my only sister, Velinda Jean Simmons, for being family and true inspirations. To the dearest loves of my life, Amber and Celeste, you made me a better human through the act of mothering. I love you deeply and dearly. To all the Ashevillians who read my poetry and attended my performances and claimed me as their own, when all my life, I have always been the edge dweller, thank you for dancing with me through these seasons *Under the Sun*.

Glenis Redmond